Hydro's Adventure
Through the Water Cycle

Written by
Randi and Michael Goodrich

Illustrations by
Michele Han

GeoQuest Publications
Lake Oswego, Oregon

Hydro's Adventure Through the Water Cycle
by Randi and Michael Goodrich

Published by:
GeoQuest Publications
P.O. Box 1665
Lake Oswego, Oregon 97035-1212 U.S.A.
www.geoquest.net

Editor: Joan Maiers
Cover and Interior Illustrations: Michele Han
Graphic Design: Kendra Hume Design
Publications Consultation: Carolyn Buan

First Printing
Printed in China by C & C Offset Printing Co., Ltd.

Publisher's Cataloging-in-Publication
(Provided by Quality Books, Inc.)
Goodrich, Randi.
    Hydro's adventure through the water cycle / written by Randi and Michael Goodrich ; cover and interior illustrations by Michele Han.
        p. cm.
    Includes bibliographical references and index.
    SUMMARY: Hydro, a water molecule on the move, introduces the hydrologic cycle and explains why it's important to keep water clean as he changes states from solid to liquid to gas.
    Audience: Ages 7-12
    ISBN 0-9651101-5-X (pbk)
    ISBN 0-9651101-6-8 (casebound)

    1. Hydrologic cycle -- Juvenile literature.
[1. Hydrologic cycle. 2. Water supply.]
I. Goodrich, Michael II. Han, Michele, ill. II. Title.

    GB848.G66 2004   551.48
                    QB102-701946

Did You Know...

Water covers two-thirds of the earth's surface.
Current/The Journal of Marine Education

Nearly a million cloud droplets make up one raindrop.
A Drop of Water

A water drop is not shaped like a teardrop.
It looks more like a hamburger bun.
Alistair B. Fraser, Emeritus Professor of Meteorology, Pennsylvania State University

An average milk cow drinks 35 gallons of water per day.
National Dairy Council

Almost half of the world's people lack access to safe
drinking water.
www.villagevoice.com/issues/0235/harkavy.php pg. 1, 8.27.02

When combined, hydrogen, an explosive gas, and oxygen, a
combustible gas, create H$_2$O, a liquid, which extinguishes fires.
Natural History Magazine, July-August 2002, Volume 111, Number 6

Once evaporated, a water molecule spends ten days in the air.
United States Environmental Protection Agency-Office of Water

All the water that will ever be is, right now.
National Geographic, October 1993

Acknowledgments

The following people contributed their expertise, time or inspiration:

Carolyn Dreiger, Hydrologist, U.S. Geological Survey
Christy Ford, Uplands Elementary School
Susan Foster, Smart Travel Press
Bill Hastie, Education Coordinator, Oregon Plan for Salmon and Watersheds,
    Oregon Governor's Office
David Heil, David Heil & Associates, Inc.
Sandra Hoyt, Lexicologist
Jacquie Jones, Stonehenge Designs
Teresa Kao, Our Town Publishing
Julie Oliver, Bryant Elementary School
George H. Taylor, State Climatologist, Oregon Climate Service
Bonnie Vorenberg, ArtAge Publications
Barb Whitaker, Ginger & Spike Publications
Matt Zaffino, Chief Meteorologist, KGW Northwest NewsChannel 8

Special thanks to Bill Nye, the Science Guy, for inspiring the phrase "molecular moment."

About the Authors

Randi and Michael Goodrich are also the authors of *A Rock Grows Up.* "We create friendly earth science for readers of all ages," say the Goodriches. Their approach provides easy access to complex subjects and honors both the scientific content and the process. Their next book will feature astronomy.

In the end we will conserve only what we love;
we will love only what we understand;
and we will understand only what we are taught.

Baba Dioum (Senegal)

Cast of Characters

Doug Fir

Solid

Gas

Liquid

Hydro

I. C. Glacier

Daphne Deer

**Grandpa
Groundwater**

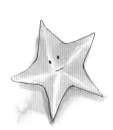

Sea Star

**Nibbler the
Salmon**

Sandy River

Hi! My name is **HydrO**! You can find me everywhere on earth — in oceans, in puddles, and in your glass of water! I'm not very big. Billions of water **molecules** like me fit in a single drop of water.

My parents are the Elements. Their first names are Oxygen and Hydrogen. Both of them are gases, but each looks very different. Oxygen is round and a real heavyweight, while Hydrogen is not only round but a definite lightweight. When the earth was young and matter existed in three states — solid, liquid and gas — my parents **bonded** and married.

I am their child. My real name is Molecular (mo-LEK-y-ler) Water, but everyone calls me **HydrO**.

CHAPTER 2

On my birthday we moved to a town called Rocky Intertidal Zone at the ocean's edge. It's a great place for leaping over rocks of all sizes and playing in tide pools. The tide pools are homes for many of my friends. Peri Winkle, a snail, lives in a taffy-colored shell house. Sea Anemone (a-NEM-o-nee) lives in a soft green house with green tentacles. Hermit Crab moves with the tides so he carries his house on his back.

Sea Star is also one of my intertidal friends. She has arms called rays, but no legs or toes. The rays are lined with hundreds of tiny, soft suction cups. They cling with such power that the crashing waves can't sweep her away. Whenever Sea Star wants to move, she sucks in some water and forces it slowly through canals in her body and out to her suction cups. This causes a shift in the water pressure and allows her to move.

All of my friends at Rocky Intertidal Zone stay in their own neighborhood, but not me. I'm a water molecule and I love to travel! You see, I'm part of the **Hydrologic Cycle** (HI-dro-loj-ik SI-cul). I can change shape and become a solid, liquid or gas. I've made friends all over the world. Plus, I get to ride the Vapor Express!

WATER CYCLE
travel guide

The Vapor Express is the train I catch when I **evaporate** (e-VAP-or-rate) and convert from a liquid to a gas. This process happens because of a change in the temperature, wind, humidity or pressure.

As I swim around the intertidal pool, the sun shines down and warms me up. Right now, I have no plans to ride the Vapor Express.

Suddenly, the wind grabs me and swirls me around the tide pool. Before I know it, I am heading out to sea.

A gust of wind hurls me and my friends into the air and plops us on top of a white, foamy wave. We're surfing! Salt particles zoom by us. We're ready to change from a liquid to a gas.

Very soon the Sun's heat breaks the bonds that join me with the other water molecules. I pull away and wave my arms.

Molecular Moment! (mo-LEK-ye-ler) (mo-Ment)

Then I spot the Vapor Express nearby. "Over here! Pick me up over here!" I shout.

The train slows down and I hop aboard. I join billions of other Sun-heated molecules. We evaporate into the air in just a few seconds. Once again, I'm a gas and up, up, up into the sky I go!

CHAPTER 4

The higher I climb the lower my temperature drops, and I change from a gas back to a liquid. I get off the Vapor Express and **condense** (KON-dens) on a small particle of dust called **Condensation Nuclei** (KON-den-say-shun) (NOO-klee-i). Then my friends and I condense together to form a cloud.

Suddenly our cloud is shoved east by the **Jet Stream**, a very strong wind. The Jet Stream develops around 30,000 feet above the ground and blows at a speed between 57 and 250 miles per hour. Traveling on the Jet Stream is like surfing in the sky!

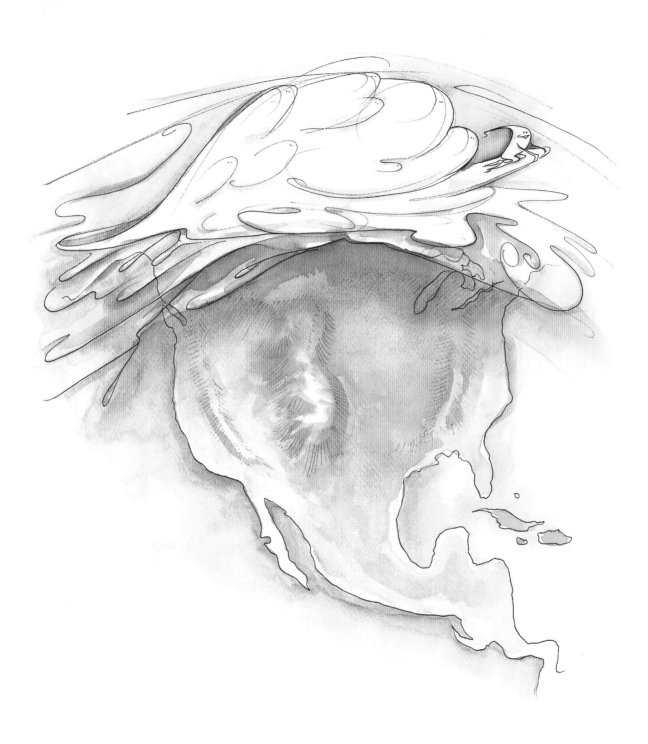

CHAPTER 5

For days, all of us in the cloud ride the Jet Stream. It carries us across the ocean and then over a huge mountain.

I really want to be a snowflake. I cling for life to the icy sides of the cloud. We climb higher and higher. I feel colder and colder. The cloud gets darker and darker.

I'm freezing! Over and over I remind myself that this is what I want. I've waited for years to become a snowflake. I must hang on till I reach the perfect temperature of minus 15 degrees Centigrade (SEN-ti-grade) or 5 degrees Fahrenheit (FAIR-en-hite).

Brrrrrrrr! I hear ice snap as it surrounds me and locks me into an ice crystal.

Then I spot another ice crystal like me.

"Will you join me in becoming a snowflake?" I ask.

"And just how do we get to be a snowflake?" asks the ice crystal as we float along.

"Oh, it's a super cool process. Snowflakes can form in a couple of ways. Either several ice crystals can freeze together or cold water droplets can collide and freeze onto an existing ice crystal. If separate ice crystals freeze together to form an icy state, this is a phase called **crystallization** (KRIS-tal-I-ZA-shun)."

I continue, "We get together and form a **hexagonal** (hex-AG-o-nal) or six-sided crystal. That's when we officially become a snowflake."

"But how do we all fit together?" asks the ice crystal.

"It's like a puzzle," I reply. "Each piece knows its proper place."

"So, how does a snowflake get its special shape?" asks the ice crystal.

"Well," I answer, "A snowflake is always six sided, but its shape can vary. In fact, over eighty different snowflake patterns exist. We never know what we'll look like until we're fully grown."

"Okay, but what happens when you land on earth? Will you just hang out, or what?"

"No, we never just hang out when we're snowflakes."

"Well, what happens?"

"Come on, I'll show you."

CHAPTER 6

We land as snowflakes on Big Mountain, a snow-capped volcano. We lie on a snowfield squished together. So much snow falls on us that we can't see the Sun.

More time passes and more snow falls. We are flattened into the **glacier**. The temperature is freezing cold.

During a blizzard, I meet a member of the Glacier family. His name is I. C. Glacier. He tells me his family covers 10 percent of the land on earth.

"How long have you been visiting here?" he asks.

I think for a minute. "Two winters, a spring and a summer."

"Well, this spring there's a good chance that you'll join the snow melt to meet up with Sandy River."

I remember how both winters on the glacier were long and cold. I have survived icequakes, thunderstorms, lightning, windstorms and blizzards. Then it was exciting, but now I'm ready to move on. When I see the spring Sun I know my river adventure is about to begin.

Suddenly I hear a loud "KRRR AK!" as the ice splits apart, and I'm on my way.

"I'm melting," I say to I. C. Glacier. "That means it's back to a liquid for me! Next, I'll travel with my cousins who live in the Sandy River."

"We'll certainly miss you, **HydrO.** But we understand. When you are part of the **water cycle** you are always on the move!"

CHAPTER 7

"Tell me again how you first got to be a creek, then a stream and then a **river**," I ask Sandy River.

She explains how any little creek can become a stream and then grow up into a river. Sandy River tells how the melted snow, rain and **groundwater** cause a stream to grow into a river. But, she adds, a river doesn't need rain or melting snow in order to grow.

"Why not?" I ask.

"Because of the groundwater," says Sandy River. "That's water that is found under the ground in the spaces between the dirt or the rock particles."

"I never knew that water traveled under my feet. How can all that dirt and rock hold water? Where do the groundwater molecules live?"

"In an **aquifer** (AK-wa-fer), which is a rock or a group of rocks whose tiny holes allow plenty of room for water. Water molecules move through the spaces in the rock. Sometimes they move several feet in just a few minutes; sometimes they take years and years to move a few inches. Soon we will be in your Grandpa Groundwater's neighborhood. We can ask him," she said.

"Great!" I say, "But right now, I want to know more about how a stream grows into a river."

"We grow by collecting rainwater, snow melt or groundwater," Sandy River replies.

CHAPTER 8

I listen as Sandy River describes how her channels fill with water. She says it's a great place for fish and people to swim. "But how do you avoid **pollution** (po-LOO-shun)?" I ask.

"It's getting harder and harder," she sighs. "If people dump chemicals or dirty water or poisonous weed killers into my system, my waters become unfit for living things."

"What kinds of living things?" I ask.

"Like fish. Fish can't live in polluted waters. The chemicals poison the fish and may reduce the oxygen content in the water."

"I didn't know that fish need oxygen just like people."

"Yes. Fish have gills to remove oxygen from the water and people have lungs to remove oxygen from the air. Certain fish, like the salmon, get their oxygen by living in a healthy flowing stream, with no pollution and lots of cold, clear water. The best salmon **environment** (en-VIRE-un-ment) is a stream with boulders, cobbles, which are about the size of your fist, some small gravel and quiet pools. Salmon also love streams with shade and tree limbs or logs. The limbs and logs create **riffles** or stretches of white-water pools. They also cause **glides**, pools of water without surface **turbulence** (TUR-bu-lens) or white water."

CHAPTER 9

The next day, I take a long nap in a quiet pool near the edge of the river. When I awake, Nibbler the Salmon is swimming nearby.

"Hi," I say to her.

"**H**ydr**O**! Sandy River! It's good to see both of you!"

"How's your family?" I ask.

Nibbler the Salmon says she and her family have felt a little too warm lately. She tells us that a healthy fish needs a water temperature of no more than 64 degrees Fahrenheit or 17.8 degrees Centigrade. If the water is too warm, the river loses oxygen and fish get sick or find it hard to breathe.

Nibbler continues, "If people let too many **nutrients**, like fertilizers, run off from their yards and farms, and if the temperature is too warm, **algae** (AL-gee) bloom. When the algae dies, the bacteria that eat the algae remove the oxygen from the river."

"We need cool water during our long journey to the sea and on our return trip home," says Nibbler. "The trees and plants along the river block direct sunlight and help keep the water cool. Without cool, clean water all the salmon suffer."

CHAPTER 10

"You're not the only one who suffers," says a voice from the riverbank.

Nibbler and I look up into the gentle face of Doug Fir.

"Hi, Doug!"

"Hello, travelers! Haven't seen you for a long, long time."

"What's new with you?" I ask.

"Plenty," says Doug Fir. "Do you have time for a few stories?"

"Sure," we reply.

Nibbler and I nestle next to Doug Fir. Our old friend, Barry Basalt, sits close by, soaking his feet in Sandy River's cool water.

Doug Fir calls a "**Flora and Fauna**" meeting and invites everyone in the Greenwood Forest to come together.

Soon a crowd of deer, raccoons and squirrels gather around Doug Fir. Then his flora neighbors, including the stately Bracken Ferns, the Sedges with edges, and the Elderberry, extend their longest and strongest branches so they too can become part of the meeting.

Some of the big trees, the Maples, the Alders and the Cottonwoods hover over Nibbler and me. This giant green umbrella forms a shield protecting us from the heat of the Sun.

Doug Fir opens the meeting by telling how polluted streams and rivers hurt all plants and animals living in or near the water. Doug Fir asks others to share their experiences. Over the next few hours, the plant and animal families who live in the Greenwood Forest share their stories about polluted streams and rivers.

An 80-foot Red Cedar tree, who is dying, is the first to speak. For 80 years her home had been along the river's edge. Some of her ancestors had lived for 800 years. When she was young, her healthy roots grew deep and wide into the rich forest soil. She stored food in her trunk. Water traveled up to her branches and leaves. Eventually it passed through her leaves to the atmosphere. This process is called **transpiration** (TRAN-spy-RAY-shun).

Over a long time the floods washed away most of the riverbank. The floods were higher and came more often now. This process exposed part of her powerful root system to the summer Sun and the winter winds. She found it harder and harder to collect nutrients from the soil near the riverbank. She lengthened her roots, but they couldn't grow fast enough and collect enough water and food to keep her healthy. No wonder she is dying.

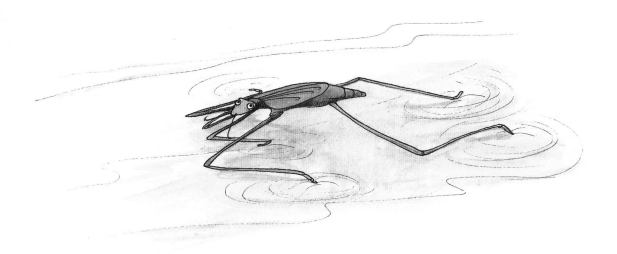

Then Daphne (DAF-nee) Deer speaks. "Animals need to drink plenty of fresh water, especially the young ones who run and play all day long. Playing is hard work! If our drinking water is unclean, my little ones will get sick or die."

"When I go to the riverbank in the morning to drink fresh water, I look for Scooter, the **water strider**. If Scooter is there, I know the drinking spot is clean and safe for my family and me. If I don't see Scooter, I look for snails or the Mayfly Nymph (NIMF) or the Stonefly Nymph. They are **aquatic** insects. They like clean water."

One after another, on a Sunday afternoon in the quiet calm of the Greenwood Forest, each creature tells a story.

And just before the sun goes down, Nibbler says to me, "Come on. I want to show you something else."

CHAPTER 11

Nibbler takes us down the river to a place called Skeleton Creek. As we draw closer, I cough and gasp and my nose starts to run. The water is so murky I can't see more than a couple of feet in front of me. And the smell is gross. Nibbler points ahead to a dark pool in the river.

"Right here, about 50 years ago," she says, "a battery shop dumped **lead** and **sulfuric acid** on the land and in the stream. All along this stream the plants and shrubs and trees have died. Today, the stream and the soil still struggle to get healthy again."

Nibbler continues, "In other places along the stream, pesticides have plugged up salmons' noses. And since salmon depend on their sense of smell to return to their home streams, this is very serious. So, if a salmon dies here, its skeleton gives warning to the other salmon."

Her story scares me.

"Let's get outta here!" I shout.

But Nibbler wants to show us one last place. We turn left and follow Nibbler as she propels herself toward a murky zone in the water. We can hardly see through the silt. Nibbler is choking for air. My chest feels tight and my nose is running.

"Why is this water so yucky?" I ask.

"Somewhere upstream all the plants and trees have been bulldozed for a new road. When the rains fall, the plants no longer hold the soil together, so it ends up in the stream. The soil clogs my gills and smothers the fish eggs that I've laid in the gravel.

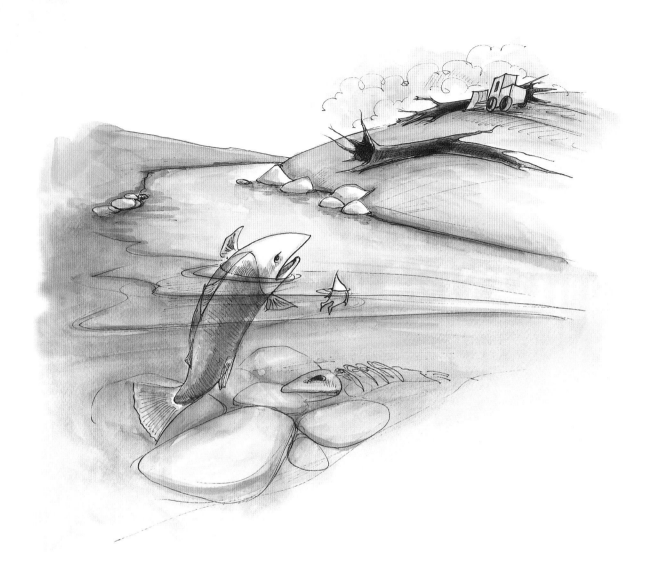

We need trees and shrubs growing along the banks of our streams and rivers to provide shade and to prevent **erosion** (e-RO-shun)."

"This clay and silt make me feel *sick*."

"Sorry, **HydrO**. I wanted you and Sandy to see why this is unhealthy water for all of us. Let's go!"

CHAPTER 12

Next we visit Pristine Pond. This is much better. My nose stops running. My chest doesn't feel tight. I can breathe again. I'm glad to get away from Skeleton Creek.

"I thought that the streams and rivers and oceans cleaned themselves, just like cats," I say.

"Nope," says Sandy River. "People need to keep us clean. If poisonous chemicals are **recycled**, they stay out of storm drains. Clean water makes everyone healthy, and it protects our communities."

Sandy River tells me how all living things depend on water, so it's very important that each tiny water molecule work hard to stay clean and healthy.

"The water cycle links together all of the earth's water with all of the earth's land," she says.

"What about smoke fumes in the air? Don't they also release poisons?" I ask.

"Sure they do. Those wastes can cause **acid rain** and the acid from that rain can get into the water. Other **toxic** chemicals in the air can get into the water in the same way."

"So pollution in one place, no matter how it gets into the water, can affect other places?" I ask.

"Yes," she says. "We all live downstream from one another, and since most streams flow into rivers, and most rivers flow into the ocean, the ocean is where the pollutants are dumped. So pollution from the streams and rivers affects the plants and animals in the ocean."

"Yuck."

"You will never die, **HydrO**, but you can get very *sick*."

"I know," I say.

CHAPTER 13

Sandy River begins to share all the stories her family told her. Then she informs me how different life is today for groundwater.

"We forget that the earth's water is about 3.8 billion years old. Today's people drink the same water that dinosaurs drank millions of years ago. We drink the same water that Christopher Columbus sailed on. It's the same water in which Native Americans netted their Salmon, and it's the same water that the Pilgrims heated for tea."

"I never thought of water like that," I say.

Then Sandy River changes her tone, "Today, groundwater is in danger."

"How come?" I ask.

"People water their lawns and that water is absorbed into the soil. Sometimes lawns are sprayed with a fertilizer, or small plants are sprayed with herbicides or pesticides. These chemicals run down the blades of grass and soak into the dirt and mix with the groundwater," Sandy River says.

"What about washing a car?" I ask.

She tells me that it's best to use a commercial car wash. Many companies recycle part of the water that's used to wash the cars. If people want to wash their own cars, it's best to use stream friendly products or waterless technology.

"Have you ever watched an insect with long legs who walks on water?" She asks me.

"You mean Scooter?"

"Exactly. Scooter, the water strider, glides along the top of the water. He doesn't fall in because the water molecules join together to create **surface tension**. This allows Scooter to stay afloat," Sandy River says.

She continues. "But when soap and chemicals get into the river system, they ruin the surface tension. Then Scooter can't glide along the top of the water and he sinks.

"That's awful," I frown.

Sandy River looks at her watch. "Ok, **HydrO**. Let's stop for now. I need to pick up the children from school."

CHAPTER 14

"Oh, before you go, may I ask you an important question?" Sandy River nods.

"What's a **watershed**?"

"A watershed is an area of land that drains down a slope to a river or a stream," answers Sandy River.

"So, why does everybody make such a big deal about a watershed?" I ask.

"It's part of your community. If a watershed is clean and safe, so is your neighborhood," answers Sandy River. "And since watersheds connect all communities, it's important to keep your neighborhood watershed unpolluted."

"How big is a watershed?"

"There are watersheds within watersheds. That little trickle in your backyard is part of a watershed. Somewhere that little trickle flows into a stream, and the stream flows into a river and the river flows into the ocean. The trickle, the stream and the river are all part of a watershed."

CHAPTER 15

The next afternoon, I take a long nap near the edge of a little stream while Bucky Beaver and Frannie Frog play nearby. When I awake, I find myself slowly moving past some cobbles and down into the ground. It is dark and cool and crowded with lots of sand particles. It's difficult to stretch out. One minute I'm part of a little stream and then whoosh, I disappear below the surface of the earth. I'm in Grandpa Groundwater's neighborhood!

I find Grandpa Groundwater at the Liquid Lunch Deli in Aquifer reading **The Daily Ripple**. I sit down next to him and order a Watercress Salad and a Liquid Lime. I haven't seen Grandpa Groundwater for a long time.

"So, how old are you now, **HydrO**?" Grandpa asks setting the newspaper aside.

"I just had my 300th birthday," I say. "And how old are you, Grandpa?"

"Well, let's see. My last birthday as a groundwater molecule was around the time that Leif Ericson came from Norway to discover America in the year 1000. So that means I'm over a thousand years old."

"Is that why you move so slowly?"

"Slowly? Why I move a foot a day. But if you think that's slow, listen to this! My Egyptian Sandstone Cousin is 40,000 years old. He was old when the Pyramids were built! If you think I'm slow, **HydrO**, this cousin moves less than an inch a year. That's because the drier the climate, the slower groundwater moves."

"How did you get into the Groundwater Family? I mean, why aren't you Steam or Rain or Seawater?"

"You know, that's what's so great about life as a water molecule," Grandpa answers. "I am all of these, but not at the same time. For awhile, I'm a solid molecule. Then I can convert to a liquid molecule. After that I may evaporate and catch the Vapor Express! It just depends on my place in the Hydrologic Cycle."

"But back to your question," Grandpa continues. "Over a thousand years ago, I lived in the Pacific Ocean. I remember the exact day when my time came to catch the Vapor Express and evaporate."

"What happened?" I ask, inching closer.

"Well, the Sun grew very hot, which made me absorb more and more energy. When I had the right amount of energy, I evaporated. I broke away from the other seawater molecules and flew into the air. I was invisible!"

Grandpa continues, "I climbed higher and higher into the atmosphere. Then I got colder and colder. I lost some of my energy. I floated around for awhile until I bumped into other molecules. Soon **zillions** of us bumped into one another. We clung together long enough to find a tiny piece of salt from the sea breeze and hopped aboard. This process made us into droplets of water. Then we fell to the earth's surface in the form of rain. I lived in the river until I moved to Aquifer."

I looked at my Grandpa's white hair, big bushy eyebrows and twinkling eyes. For a thousand-year-old molecule, he is well preserved.

I ask him how big the Groundwater Family is.

"Well, let's see," says Grandpa, rubbing his chin with his hand. "Think about all the fresh water on the earth."

"Hmmm. Yeah. Okay," I say.

"Now multiply that by 60. That's how much Groundwater is here under the earth's surface, and that's how big the Groundwater Family is."

"Whoa!" I sigh, closing my eyes and trying to imagine all that water.

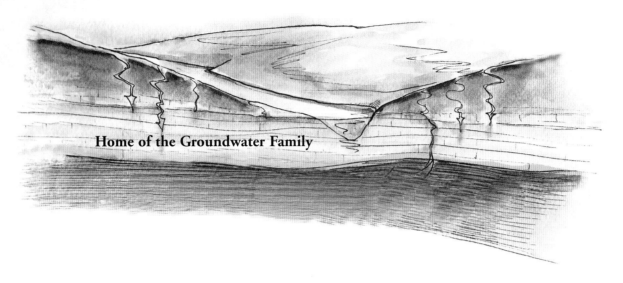

Home of the Groundwater Family

"How did the family get there?" I ask Grandpa.

"Groundwater comes from many sources. When it rains or snows, the water soaks into the ground. Also some groundwater comes from lakes and rivers."

"Is groundwater still part of the water cycle, even though it's below the ground?" I ask.

"Oh, yes. All water on the earth is part of the Hydrologic Cycle; whether it's groundwater, rainwater, snow, part of an animal or plant or perspiration, it's all part of the cycle. Yes, indeed, groundwater is part of the cycle. Since groundwater can flow in any direction, eventually it finds its way to the surface of the earth. At the place where groundwater flows out of the ground, it becomes a spring. Finally it will become part of a river or stream."

"I guess when water moves through an aquifer it doesn't have much wiggle room, so a groundwater molecule finds it hard to move from one place to another," I say.

"That's right," replies Grandpa. "The wiggle room depends on whatever is under the ground. Just look around. Here at the Liquid Lunch Deli, there's plenty of headroom. But once we're outside, the streets are narrow and the buildings have low ceilings."

Grandpa continues, "Imagine that an aquifer is like a sandbox. When a bucket of water empties over the sandbox, the water disappears between each of the tiny grains of sand."

"Out of sight!" I laugh.

"Right!" he says, his eyes twinkling at my quick response.

"Now it's exactly the same idea with an aquifer. An aquifer is made from sand, gravel or limestone. When water disappears into the ground, it collects in an aquifer."

"Like a sponge?" I ask.

"Yes. An aquifer is similar to a sponge. And just like a sponge, it can soak up only a certain amount of water. If the aquifer is too full, the water oozes out to the surface of the earth. Then it's no longer groundwater but surface water."

Grandpa continues, "You know how all those tiny holes in a sponge are connected with secret passageways? It's the same with an aquifer, except that some of those holes and passageways have more wiggle room than others. The liquid water molecules continually move and flow in many directions. Sometimes there is lots of wiggle room and sometimes very little. It depends on the location of the molecules."

I am curious about how fast the groundwater molecule could travel, and Grandpa tells me its speed depends on two things. The first is how **porous** the rock or soil is, and the second is how much **pressure** pushes down on the aquifer. If there is too much pressure from the rocks above, he says, the aquifer can't hold as much water.

"Then what happens?" I ask.

"Think again of the sponge," he says. "What happens when you take your hand and squeeze it?"

I pictured the sponge. "Well, if I squeeze it gently, the water flows out slowly. But if I squeeze it as hard as I can, the water pours out quickly. I guess that means that with more pressure, the water moves faster. Less pressure means less movement."

"Molecular Moment!" laughs Grandpa.

CHAPTER 16

One day I receive a letter from Sea Star. She has missed surfing with me and asks when I planned to move back to the beach. I miss Sea Star too, so I call her.

When Sea Star answers the phone, I say "Hi! It's **HydrO**."

"Hey! Where are you?"

"Aquifer."

"When are you coming home?"

"I don't know."

"Why?"

"Sea Star, remember I am a water molecule and part of the hydrologic cycle. My home is everywhere. I never know when I'll return to a certain place."

"Can you speed up the process in the cycle?"

"No, that's the Sun's job."

"But I want to celebrate your birthday with you. I thought we could go surfing together."

"Sounds good," I said. "But the most I can promise is a strong maybe."

"What do you mean?"

"Since I'm part of a cycle, there's no beginning. There's no ending. For awhile I spend time as a liquid molecule swimming and surfing with you in the ocean. Then I evaporate into a gas molecule and play bumper cars with my drippy friends on the cloud. When the time is right, I catch the Gravity Express heading back to earth, where I turn into a solid piece of ice. I land on the mountain and slide back through a wintry life."

"Then one spring day, I loosen up and shake off the ice. I melt into the river and either flow into the ocean or get pulled into the ground as part of an aquifer. When I'm at the surface I get whooshed away by the heat of the sun. That's when the earth's hydrologic cycle starts all over again."

CHAPTER 17

Right then and there it occurs to me! All the **gazillions** of tiny water molecules like me make the Earth different from other planets in the Solar System. It's the water! The water! It's the lakes, the rivers and the oceans! It's the rain, the snow and the hail! It's the condensation, evaporation and **precipitation** (pre-sip-i-TAH-shun)! Without water, Earth is a planet where nothing can live. Without water, there are no oceans, no clouds, no snow-covered mountains. Without water there is no me. Without water there is no you.

"Well, **HydrO**," says Sea Star, I'll see you around when I see you."

"Molecular Moment!"

Dear Readers,

When you pour a drink of water,
it's an ordinary experience.
Water is there.
Always there.
            Until it's not...
Then, a drink of water
is an extraordinary experience.

Hydro

Glossary

Acid Rain	(AS-id) Rain, sleet, snow or wet precipitation that contains sulfuric acid and nitric acid. It forms when water vapor reacts with particular chemical compounds.
Algae	(AL-gee) Plants that live in ponds, rivers, lakes, oceans or moist soil.
Aquatic	(a-KWAT-ik) Living or growing in or on the water.
Aquifer	(AK-wa-fer) An underground body of sediment or rock with spaces that can hold a useful amount of water. Aquifers vary in capacity and size.
Bonded	Held together by a uniting force or tie.
Condense	(KON-dens) To change into a denser form such as a gas to a liquid, or steam into water.
Condensation Nuclei	(KON-den-SAY-shun) (NOO-klee-i) Particles in the air such as dust, ash, pollen or sea salt on which water vapor can condense.
Crystallization	(KRIS-tal-i-ZA-shun) The process of forming a solid structure with similar molecules. Snowflakes and rock crystals are an example.
Environment	(en-VIRE-un-ment) Everything that surrounds people including plants, animals, weather and buildings.
Erosion	(e-RO-shun) The natural processes of the wearing away of the land by wind, water and glaciers.
Evaporate	(e-VAP-or-ate) Water changes from a liquid state to a gas (or vapor state) when an energy like the Sun heats it to a certain temperature.

Fauna	(FAW-nuh) Animal life characteristic of a certain region and time period.
Flora	Plant life characteristic of a certain region and time period.
Gazillions	Millions and millions and millions.
Glacier	A large mass of freshwater ice flowing slowly over land.
Glides	Areas of fast moving water with a smooth surface.
Groundwater	Water stored beneath the earth's surface in the spaces in the soil and underground rocks. Accumulates mainly from rain and melted snow and from water that seeps into the ground from lakes and ponds.
Hexagonal	(hex-AG-o-nal) Having six angles and six sides.
Hydrologic Cycle	(HI-dro-loj-ik) (SI-cul) The never-ending flow of water among oceans, rivers, lakes, glaciers, groundwater and the atmosphere.
Jet Stream	A narrow, horizontal stream of air current that moves between 57 and 250 miles per hour.
Lead	(led) A naturally occurring blue-gray, soft metal found in the earth's crust. Modern research proves that it can harm people, plants and animals.
Molecule	(mol-i-kyool) The smallest and most basic unit of matter.
Molecular Moment	(mo-LEK-ye-ler) (mo-Ment) The exact second when you understand something!

Nutrients	(NOO-tree-untz) Things that nourish or promote growth.
Pollution	(po-LOO-shun) Damage to the environment that is caused by toxic chemicals and garbage.
Porous	(POR-es) Having tiny openings or passageways.
Precipitation	(pre-sip-i-TAH-shun) All forms of water particles, such as rain, snow, sleet and hail that fall from clouds and reach the ground.
Pressure	(PRESH-er) A force applied over a surface.
Recycle	(re-SI-kel) To use again.
Riffle	(RIF-L) A shallow area of choppy surface water.
River	A natural stream of water that is fed by smaller streams or tributaries and empties into another body of water such as a lake or ocean.
Sulfuric Acid	(sul-FYOOR-ik) (AS-id) A dense, corrosive, oily liquid.
Surface tension	The construction of the surface of a liquid so that it contracts to behave like stretched elastic film.
Toxic	Poisonous.
Transpiration	(TRAN-spy-RAY-shun) In plants, a process that carries unused moisture from the roots to the surface of the leaves where it is released to the atmosphere.
Turbulence	(TUR-bu-lens) Irregular movements in smoothly flowing water.
Watershed	A region that drains into a river, river system or a body of water.

Water Cycle	See Hydrologic Cycle.
Water Strider	Also known as a water skipper. This long-legged member of the insect family *Gerridae* (JER-ri-dee) moves about on the surface of the water.
Zillions	Millions and millions.

Bibliography

Ahrens, C. Donald. Meteorology Today: *An Introduction to Weather, Climate, and the Environment.* Pacific Grove, CA: Brooks/Cole, 2000.

Cole, Joanna. *The Magic School Bus at the Waterworks.* New York: Scholastic, Inc., 1986.

Childs, Craig. *The Secret Knowledge of Water: Discovering the Essence of the American Desert.* Seattle: Sasquatch Books, 2000.

Geer, Ira W., Ed. *Glossary of Weather and Climate with Related Oceanic and Hydrologic Terms.* Boston: American Meteorological Society, 1996.

Leopold, Luna B. *A View of the River.* Cambridge, Mass.: Harvard University Press, 1994.

Nicholas, Jay W. *Down to the Sea: The Story of a Little Salmon and His Neighborhood.* Wilsonville: Book Partners, Inc., 1994.

Nye, Bill, Erren Gottlieb and James McKenna. (1996). *Bill Nye the Science Guy: Water Cycle/Oceanography* [Television Series Episode]. Elk Grove Village, Illinois: Disney Educational Productions.

Outwater, Alice. *Water: A Natural History.* New York: Basic Books, 1996.

Pielou, E. C. *Fresh Water.* Chicago: The University of Chicago Press, 1998.

Robbins, Elaine. "Our Water, Ourselves." *E/The Environmental Magazine IX, Number 5* (1998): 28-35.

Sagan, Carl and Ann Druyan. *Shadows of Forgotten Ancestors.* New York: Ballantine Books, 1992.

Spellman, Frank R. *The Science of Water: Concepts and Applications.* Lancaster, Penn.: Technomic Publishing Co., Inc., 1998.

Susuki, David. *Looking at Weather.* New York: John Wiley & Sons, Inc., 1991.

Wick, Walter. *A Drop of Water: A Book of Science and Wonder.* New York: Scholastic Press, 1997.

Index

Give the Gift of an Extraordinary Science Story

Complete this form and mail it with your check,
credit card or purchase order information to:

GeoQuest Publications
P.O. Box 1665
Lake Oswego, OR 97035-1212
www.geoquest.net
Email: info@geoquest.net

Please send _____ softcover copies of
Hydro's Adventure Through the Water Cycle at $17.95 each. $ _____

Please send _____ hardcover copies of
Hydro's Adventure Through the Water Cycle at $24.95 each. $ _____

Please send _____ softcover copies of *A Rock Grows Up:*
The Pacific Northwest Up Close and Personal at $9.95 each. $ _____

                                                                    Total $ _____

Name _____

Address_____

City _____ State _____ Zip_____

Telephone _____ Email _____

I understand that I may return the book for a full refund for any reason. No questions asked.

SHIPPING:

- Orders up to $30: add $5.00
- Orders $30-$50: add $7.50
- Orders $50-$100: add $10.00
- Rush Orders: add $10
- International Orders: add $10

PAYMENT: Check, Credit Card or Purchase Order
Checks and money orders payable in U.S. dollars only

Books $_____
Shipping $_____
Total $_____   Check for $ _____ enclosed

CREDIT CARD: We accept VISA and MasterCard

Card Number _____ Exp. Date _____

Name on Card _____